Same as Me

A Collection of Poems

Heather Helene Hulett

Copyright © 2019 by Heather Helene Hulett

All rights reserved. This book or any portion thereof may not be reproduced or used in any manner whatsoever without the express written permission of the publisher except for the use of brief quotations in a book review.

Printed in the United States of America.

ISBN: 978-0-578-43390-5

Table of Contents

Same as Me
1

Four Seasons of Love
5

I Remember You
7

Talk To Me
9

Safe Zone
11

The Purple Flower
13

A Simple Dimple
15

Unconditionally
17

Nothing You Could Do
19

Numb
21

Damsel in Distress
23

Accidentally in Love
25

Poetry
27

Charlie
29

Magic Words
31

Fading into Dawn
33

Spirited Ink
35

Out of Time
37

More than Love
39

Holding Space
41

Swimming through Time
43

Pain Manifested
45

Never Not
47

Two Hearts One Book
49

Connection
51

Pieces
57

Temporary
57

Mislead
59

In a Dream
61

Peace
63

A Note From the Author

I must take a moment to say thank you. To genuinely thank the beautiful souls that inspired me to write the poems contained within. The souls that have healed my heart and the souls that have broken it, the souls that are still with me and the souls that have moved on. Each, truly bringing out the best possible version of me. I cannot imagine a more beautiful offering. For it is in the depths of these extraordinary emotions I have come to find the most precious gifts. These gifts become a part of me, the pieces that make up the whole. I believe we are not so different, in fact much the same. Deep inside, I truly think, there are others who can relate to a similar fate. I offer up the pieces of my heart, in the hope that you will see, you are, in fact, the same as me. I love you all eternally.

Same as You

I wish things could be different
I wish I never knew
Just how much can be affected
By one the same as you

It must have seemed impossible
But nothing ever is
We were tempted to surrender
In fact, we almost did

Although the words unspoken
They never needed be
I know you felt me in your heart
And you too I a dream

Perhaps it wasn't special
Tell this thy self I will
For nothing has compared
To how you made me feel

That something special in your eyes
It touched my soul for sure
A heart that matched my own in time
But touch, it never will
We have no choices, just this one
Though both will be impacted

Know this I do and don't regret
For all I've learned impassioned

You'll never know how much you meant
Or what you did for me
You were a beacon in the dark
I know God sent to me

Will carry you with me through time
You're now a part of me
Each passing day I'll miss you so
But thankful always be
For lucky I have been you see
To find someone the same as me

I wish I could have kept you
God knows this to be true
For all I would have given
Just to be with you

My heart says stay
My head says go
But God he wins the race
So carry you with me I will
Forever in this place

God help me in discerning
God take despair away
Cause nothing can be done
Without you to guide the way

I wish things could be different
I wish I never knew
Just how much can be affected
By one the same as you

Four Seasons of Love

I've wished to see the spring with you.
To feel it on your skin.
And when the heat of summer comes
It is the rain I'd wrap you in.

But what of winter when it shows
How harsh and lonely.
I'd travel to the moon
And beg the sun to shine on thee.

Oh let us not forget the fall
How magical and free.
It's here that I could show you things
You never would believe.

I Remember You

I remember you.
I remember you I say.
It wasn't your face, your eyes, or smile.
It wasn't your laugh, your wit, or charm.

I remember you.
I remember you I say.
It was your soul mine recognized.
It was my heart that sent for thee.

It knows when it is needed.
It knows when to go away.
But something tells me,
In this place,
We were simply meant to stay.

Talk to Me

Talk to me about the weather.
Tell me is it beautiful?
Or is it stormy altogether,
The constant rain of rise and fall?

Talk to me about the earth.
Tell me is it round and free?
Or does it just go on forever,
Imagining what we will be?

Talk to me about the sky.
Tell me is it majesty?
Or does it simply stay in place,
Forever watching over thee?

Talk to me about the moon.
Tell me is it lovely?
Or does it miss the rays of light,
It's sacrifice for all to see?

Now talk to me about the sun.
Tell me is it crazy?
Or does it simply light the way,
So you can find your way to me?

Safe Zone

Your pedestal beyond my reach,
Though strained to touch I've tried.

Perhaps it's more the thought of you,
So perfect in my eyes.

My safe zone I do call you,
Not knowing really why.

To live within this fantasy,
Is killing me inside.

The Purple Flower

Raindrops of blue glass,
The purple flower ponders.
Infinite in its colors,
All blended in a mess.

Its walls they do constrain,
The limits always pressed.
Waiting to escape it all,
But knowing what is best.

A Simple Dimple

Your hugs are like a tidal wave,
I feel them in my core.
Foundation trembles at your touch,
That leaves me wanting more.

You are the right and I the left,
A simple dimple I adore.
His body pressed against my own,
I let my hands explore.

You pull me close and I submit,
My body is all yours.
His warmth is felt deep in my bones,
I feel like I could soar.

You make me come alive inside,
My breath I give to thee.
He feels it to and moans with me,
I gasp and must implore.

But time is up,
The clock strikes 8,
It's time for me to go.
Was just a dream,
A Fantasy,
That I cannot ignore.

Unconditionally

Give up the ghost
I surely will
Though haunting it will be.

Truth be told
I must admit
I never thought you'd see.

Out of sight
But never mind
The door you've shown to me.

Was so confused
Although I tried
Could never find the key.

So long my friend
Lost hope I have
A fool I'm shown to be.

Was this the way
It had to be?
So much for unconditionally.

Nothing You Could Do

So long ago I told you this.
There's nothing you could do.
With all my heart I do convey.
I hope you know it's true.

The center of my heart is yours,
Just waiting in a line.
I ask for nothing but just this,
Please stay with me through time.

Numb

Don't want to feel
Just want to run.
Can't help but be
Completely numb.

Don't want to stay
Just want to go.
The problem is
No one's at home.

I've said goodbye
Just walked away.
Now tell my heart
To let it stay.

Damsel in Distress

I don't believe in magic,
At least I never did.

I don't believe in fairy tales,
Not since I was a kid.

No knight in shining armor,
No damsel in distress.

No one out there to rescue,
Such a God forsaken mess.

Accidentally in Love

Shut it off, I tell myself,
You're not allowed this love.
A weight that sits upon my chest,
If only it would budge.

My mind won't stop,
It's haunting me.
When will it just be through?

I bid my heart to beat again,
For something more than you.
Blinded it has been,
Forever holding true.

Poetry

Oh how it made my heart happy
And I could image in those moments
Of reading it,
These were the words of my love,
Speaking just to me.

Charlie

With the wind in his hair
He rode toward the west.
If only he'd known
He'd take his last breathe.

The sun was high
And the air was thick.
Broken woman at the wheel
Grim reaper makes his pick.

In a flash it was over
And the dust settled down.
What was left only memories
And a wound left unbound.

Magic Words

Words…Never enough of them…often too many.

I do all the talking.
I wonder why that is?
Perhaps you do not need me.
Perhaps you never did.

You hide behind your magic.
I wish you'd share with me.
Perhaps the words escape you.
Perhaps you wish they did.

Fading into Dawn

We used to talk so often
But now it seems you've gone.
I so hoped that you'd soften
And see that we are drawn.

Alas I must move on now
So tired of this place.
The dawn it comes to bargain
And I cannot keep pace.

Spirited Ink

Printed on your heart they say
That special one for me.
I must confess, did not believe
Until the day he came to me.
My heart it knew,
My soul sky high.
How could this even be?
The time had come to finally see
My heart had always belong to He.

Out of Time

My heart it hurts
It yearns for him
Can barely hold the pen.

So angry at my heart
It's deceiving never ends!

Let him go
I beg
I plead
Or finish me
It will indeed!

Feel someone else
I pray to thee
Let him go away.

Not out of sight
Or out of mind
But out of heart
And out of time!

More than Love

There is a language,
It is little known.
It bridges gaps,
No bounds it knows.
It reaches further than the mile,
Is shared between just two.

Two hearts that beat,
As if were one.
Exchange remain unseen.
For only those,
With soul to bear
Will ever really see.
A heart that sparks
For only one
Without a word is key.

This language understood somehow
Divinity ensured
Will recognize for whom it yearns.
No effort is required here
Is almost magical.
The stamp imprinted on the heart,
The language
More than love.

Holding Space

Some spaces
Can only be filled
By the soul
They were created for.

Swimming through Time

I feel my heart is lost
Somewhere out there in space
And I must keep on swimming
Forever looking for his Grace.

Pain Manifested

Why do we look upon our tears
After wiping them from our face?
Perhaps it is simply surprise
The physical manifestation
Our pain has suddenly produced.
Indeed they take a life their own
Trickling down our cheeks
To fall into our palm.

Never Not

Should have been
More traumatized.
I somehow though
Was not.
The hand of God
Protected me,
Forever,
Never not.

Two Hearts One Book

I'm losing you
Or so it seems.
I never could quite grasp
Just what you were supposed to mean
Perhaps the time has passed.

Held on so tight
And for dear life
Cause nothing could compare.

If test it be
I failed indeed
One touch was all
It took.

I feel it now
Though days long past
My destiny he shook.

One human that I barely knew
Two hearts and just one book.
The best and worst brought out in me
With just a simple look.
Must find a way to say farewell
Before I'm undertook.

Connection

Our consistent inability to effectively communicate with one another face to face has implicitly destroyed the basic human connection.

It is the eyes that show us things.
Not words upon a screen.
It is the same
We all yearn for.
A soul connection
with another human being.

Pieces

I could not compete.
I refuse to even try.
As my heart says goodbye
I tremble inside.
God you were special
Just wanted to know
Why?

Am so very angry
Why is this so?
Only wanted to know
Can we connect
At the soul?

Oh, you will know
But it will kill you
In doing so.
You will see it
You will feel it
You will know it is there.
Expect Nothing
Short of despair.
A carrot that dangles
Just out of reach.
A bright future
With nothing to teach.

Get used to it
Closure just preaches.
To whom we are destined
To hand out our pieces.

Temporary

What a façade
This life that you live
Your eyes rodomontade
Your behavior captive.

Do not you grow weary?
That heart must be restive
Always unwilling to just be receptive.

It must get so old
Just pounding the stone
Never stepping outside of the comfort zone
Forever searching for passion unknown.

Please don't get lost
Sitting upon your throne.
Remember our lives
On temporary loan
And happiness my friend
Very dangerous to postpone.

Mislead

Do not listen
To the world
As it screams
It is lies.

The heart
It knows
The difference
The soul
Can not
Deny.

In a Dream

In a dream
I felt your flesh
I held your hand
I tasted your breathe.

In a dream
I loved you true
I sacrificed
I came to you.

In a dream
You made me feel
You made me see
You changed my reality.

In a dream
Where I wish to be
Is just exactly
The most satisfactory
Grand finale.

Peace

So here we are.
It's a peaceful place.
I carry you with me
In an unknown space.

It's been a long journey
But we both agree
There are things more important
Than our own selfish needs.

The interesting thing,
I've stumbled upon.
The love that is shared
Will never be gone.

I've spoken before
These spaces we make.
Finally realizing
All it takes is just faith.

About the Author

Heather Helene Hulett is an accomplished fortune 500 Business Analyst by day and a passionate writer by night. She spent her early years split between the mountains of Montana and the flat lands of Kansas, currently residing in the sunflower state. She earned both her bachelor and Master's degrees from Wichita State University which propelled her into the world of business and professional writing. Her education and life experience offered a unique opportunity to find and touch similar hearts. Her mission is to shine a light on the darkness that so often accompanies pain, loss and tragedy. To help those who may feel lost in the shadows to find and feel their way out.

Having faced death, her own mortality and great tragedy from an early age, Heather turned to writing. She found that poetry, philosophy and the written word, not only provided a space to heal but also a platform to reach other hearts living in similar tragedy and circumstance. Her writing began as a selfish mechanism to somehow simply survive the pain and horrors that life so frequently bestows; however, her writing eventually manifested into a platform, an opportunity to reach and help comfort others who have been dealt a similar hand in fate.

Heather has dedicated her life to loving others through their pain. She offers up the most vulnerable and even humiliating pieces of her own heart, with a humble faith that someone, somewhere will be impacted positively and they too can navigate their way through the dark.

www.ingramcontent.com/pod-product-compliance
Lightning Source LLC
Chambersburg PA
CBHW021959290426
44108CB00012B/1130